Revive Our Hearts™

ABIGAIL

LIVING WITH THE DIFFICULT PEOPLE IN YOUR LIFE

A Bible study based
on the teaching of

———

NANCY DeMOSS
WOLGEMUTH

© 2018 by *Revive Our Hearts*
Second printing, 2019

Published by *Revive Our Hearts*
P.O. Box 2000, Niles, MI 49120

ISBN: 978-1-934718-68-1

Printed in the United States of America.

Adapted from the teaching of Nancy DeMoss Wolgemuth by Mindy Kroesche, Micayla Greathouse, and Leanna Shepard, edited by Hayley Mullins and Erin Davis.

As you work through this study, use this space to doodle, color, and meditate on God's Word and consider how the account of Abigail's life gives you true hope.

FOR WHATEVER WAS WRITTEN IN FORMER DAYS WAS WRITTEN FOR OUR INSTRUCTION *THAT THROUGH endurance & THROUGH THE encouragement OF THE Scriptures WE MIGHT HAVE hope.* ROMANS 15:4

1 Samuel 25

[1] Now Samuel died. And all Israel assembled and mourned for him, and they buried him in his house at Ramah.

DAVID AND ABIGAIL

Then David rose and went down to the wilderness of Paran. [2] And there was a man in Maon whose business was in Carmel. The man was very rich; he had three thousand sheep and a thousand goats. He was shearing his sheep in Carmel. [3] Now the name of the man was Nabal, and the name of his wife Abigail. The woman was discerning and beautiful, but the man was harsh and badly behaved; he was a Calebite. [4] David heard in the wilderness that Nabal was shearing his sheep. [5] So David sent ten young men. And David said to the young men, "Go up to Carmel, and go to Nabal and greet him in my name. [6] And thus you shall greet him: 'Peace be to you, and peace be to your house, and peace be to all that you have. [7] I hear that you have shearers. Now your shepherds have been with us, and we did them no harm, and they missed nothing all the time they were in Carmel. [8] Ask your young men, and they will tell you. Therefore let my young men find favor in your eyes, for we come on a feast day. Please give whatever you have at hand to your servants and to your son David.'"

⁹ When David's young men came, they said all this to Nabal in the name of David, and then they waited. ¹⁰ And Nabal answered David's servants, "Who is David? Who is the son of Jesse? There are many servants these days who are breaking away from their masters. ¹¹ Shall I take my bread and my water and my meat that I have killed for my shearers and give it to men who come from I do not know where?" ¹² So David's young men turned away and came back and told him all this. ¹³ And David said to his men, "Every man strap on his sword!" And every man of them strapped on his sword. David also strapped on his sword. And about four hundred men went up after David, while two hundred remained with the baggage.

¹⁴ But one of the young men told Abigail, Nabal's wife, "Behold, David sent messengers out of the wilderness to greet our master, and he railed at them. ¹⁵ Yet the men were very good to us, and we suffered no harm, and we did not miss anything when we were in the fields, as long as we went with them. ¹⁶ They were a wall to us both by night and by day, all the while we were with them keeping the sheep. ¹⁷ Now therefore know this and consider what you should do, for harm is determined against our master and against all his house, and he is such a worthless man that one cannot speak to him."

¹⁸ Then Abigail made haste and took two hundred loaves and two skins of wine and five sheep already prepared and five seahs of parched grain and a hundred clusters of raisins and two hundred cakes of figs, and laid them on donkeys. ¹⁹ And she said to her young men, "Go on before me; behold, I come after you." But she did not tell her husband Nabal. ²⁰ And as she rode on the donkey and came down under cover of the mountain, behold, David and his men came down toward her, and she met them. ²¹ Now David had said, "Surely in vain have I guarded all that this fellow has in the wilderness, so that nothing was missed of all that belonged to him, and he has returned me evil for good. ²² God do so to the enemies of David and more also, if by morning I leave so much as one male of all who belong to him."

²³ When Abigail saw David, she hurried and got down from the donkey and fell before David on her face and bowed to the ground. ²⁴ She fell at his feet and said, "On me alone, my lord, be the guilt.

Please let your servant speak in your ears, and hear the words of your servant. ²⁵ Let not my lord regard this worthless fellow, Nabal, for as his name is, so is he. Nabal is his name, and folly is with him. But I your servant did not see the young men of my lord, whom you sent. ²⁶ Now then, my lord, as the Lord lives, and as your soul lives, because the Lord has restrained you from bloodguilt and from saving with your own hand, now then let your enemies and those who seek to do evil to my lord be as Nabal. ²⁷ And now let this present that your servant has brought to my lord be given to the young men who follow my lord. ²⁸ Please forgive the trespass of your servant. For the Lord will certainly make my lord a sure house, because my lord is fighting the battles of the Lord, and evil shall not be found in you so long as you live. ²⁹ If men rise up to pursue you and to seek your life, the life of my lord shall be bound in the bundle of the living in the care of the Lord your God. And the lives of your enemies he shall sling out as from the hollow of a sling. ³⁰ And when the Lord has done to my lord according to all the good that he has spoken concerning you and has appointed you prince over Israel, ³¹ my lord shall have no cause of grief or pangs of conscience for having shed blood without cause or for my lord working salvation himself. And when the Lord has dealt well with my lord, then remember your servant."

³² And David said to Abigail, "Blessed be the Lord, the God of Israel, who sent you this day to meet me! ³³ Blessed be your discretion, and blessed be you, who have kept me this day from bloodguilt and from working salvation with my own hand! ³⁴ For as surely as the Lord, the God of Israel, lives, who has restrained me from hurting you, unless you had hurried and come to meet me, truly by morning there had not been left to Nabal so much as one male." ³⁵ Then David received from her hand what she had brought him. And he said to her, "Go up in peace to your house. See, I have obeyed your voice, and I have granted your petition."

³⁶ And Abigail came to Nabal, and behold, he was holding a feast in his house, like the feast of a king. And Nabal's heart was merry within him, for he was very drunk. So she told him nothing at all until the morning light. ³⁷ In the morning, when the wine had gone out of Nabal, his wife told him these things, and his heart died within him, and

he became as a stone. [38] And about ten days later the Lord struck Nabal, and he died. [39] When David heard that Nabal was dead, he said, "Blessed be the Lord who has avenged the insult I received at the hand of Nabal, and has kept back his servant from wrongdoing. The Lord has returned the evil of Nabal on his own head." Then David sent and spoke to Abigail, to take her as his wife. [40] When the servants of David came to Abigail at Carmel, they said to her, "David has sent us to you to take you to him as his wife." [41] And she rose and bowed with her face to the ground and said, "Behold, your handmaid is a servant to wash the feet of the servants of my lord." [42] And Abigail hurried and rose and mounted a donkey, and her five young women attended her. She followed the messengers of David and became his wife.

[43] David also took Ahinoam of Jezreel, and both of them became his wives. [44] Saul had given Michal his daughter, David's wife, to Palti the son of Laish, who was of Gallim.

Many of the letters and emails we receive at *Revive Our Hearts* are from women feeling trapped in a difficult or impossible situation.

For some, it's their marriage. They're married to a man who is impossible to love, humanly speaking. Or perhaps it's a situation at work—a boss or coworker they can't please. It may even be someone they can't get along with in their church.

You might have one of those difficult people in your home, workplace, church, neighborhood, or somewhere else. The question is, how do you live with these kinds of people? How do you respond with wisdom when you're dealing with someone who is ungodly or foolish?

First Samuel 25 tells an amazing story of an extraordinary woman who did just that. She's not as well-known as some of the other women in the Bible like Mary of Nazareth or Deborah or Sarah. But this woman, Abigail, has so much to teach us through the example of her life.

As we go through this study, we will also study two other main characters in this passage. At any given time in your life, you may relate to any one of these three people. So as we look at their examples, we want to see what God has to teach us for our own lives.

TIPS FOR USING THIS STUDY

When you do a character study in the Bible, it helps to determine whether the person is giving a good or bad example to follow. Throughout this study, ask yourself these questions:

- Is there an example for me to either follow or avoid? If so, what?
- What do this passage and these people teach me about the heart, the ways, and the character of God?
- How does this passage point to Jesus and the gospel?

At the end of our six weeks, we will revisit these questions as we review what God has taught us about our lives, how He wants us to live out the gospel in specific situations, and most importantly, about His heart and His character.

As you go throughout the study, you may find it beneficial to listen to the accompanying audio series, "Abigail: How to Live with the Fools in Your Life." Find it at ReviveOurHearts.com/Abigail.

Remember, the Holy Spirit is our primary teacher as we seek to understand God's Word. Jesus told us that the Holy Spirit is a gift and a "Helper" able to "teach you all things and bring to your remembrance all that I have said to you" (John 14:26).

Secondary tools that can help you better understand the Word of God (but aren't necessary to complete this study) include:

- An English dictionary to look up the basic meaning of words
- Various translations of the Bible
- A concordance
- A Bible dictionary
- Commentaries
- A study Bible
- Colored pens or pencils to write in your Bible

A PRACTICAL EXAMPLE

Note: Throughout this study, you will find fill-in-the-blank sections using the English Standard version (ESV) translation of the Bible. If you prefer a different translation, you can use an online Bible such as BibleGateway.com or a Bible app to help with these sections.

We've also included group discussion questions at the end of this study. You can further join the Abigail discussion with our *Women of the Bible* podcast created to accompany this study, available at ReviveOurHearts.com/WomenOfTheBible.

Spend time meditating on and memorizing the following verse this week:

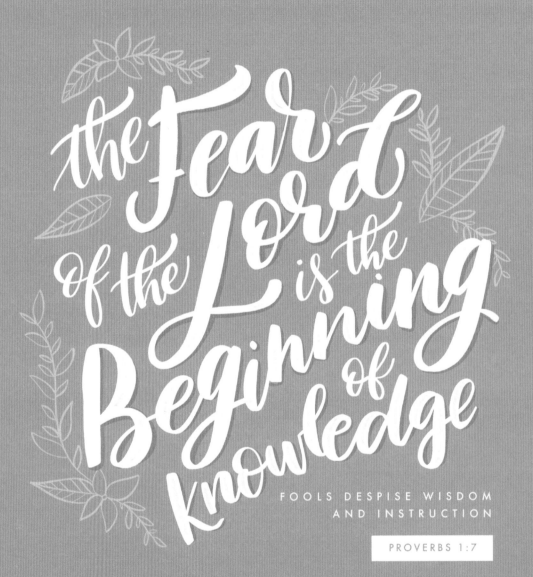

the Fear of the Lord is the Beginning of knowledge

FOOLS DESPISE WISDOM
AND INSTRUCTION

PROVERBS 1:7

Week 1

Introduction

What's in a name? All throughout the Bible, many people are introduced in the text by their name and the meaning of their name. Twins Jacob and Esau were named because of their characteristics at birth. The firstborn entered the world as a red, hairy baby, "so they named him Esau" (Gen. 25:25). Jacob received his name because he left his mother's womb grabbing Esau's heel. In the case of Abram and Sarai, God Himself renamed them Abraham and Sarah with great purpose and foreshadowing of the people that would come from them.

Names carry significance with them in Scripture, and they can sometimes be indicative of a person's nature. Long before Jesus was born, it was prophesied that His name would be Immanuel, which means "God with us" (Isa. 7; Matt. 1). He is with us indeed.

In the story of Abigail, names matter. This week we'll be looking at some individuals who lived up to their names in both good and bad ways. As we study their lives, we will learn how to relate to people with difficult characteristics.

1st SAMUEL OVERVIEW

AUTHOR

The Bible does not say who wrote 1 Samuel, but many scholars think that the prophets Samuel, Nathan, and Gad provided much of the material.

WHEN

First Samuel covers a period of 110 years, starting from the ending days of the judges, when Samuel was born (ca. 1120 BC) through the death of Saul (1011 BC).

WHERE

The entire book takes place in the land of Israel.

Day 1: A NATION IN MOURNING

Read 1 Samuel 25:1.

When President Ronald Reagan died in June 2004, the United States mourned as a nation. Flags across the country were flown at half-mast, and thousands upon thousands of people lined up—first in California and then in the streets of Washington D.C.—to stand and watch the funeral procession drive through the streets. As Reagan's body lay in state at the Capitol Rotunda, over 100,000 people stood in line (some of them for up to three hours) to file by the casket and pay their last respects.

We start off 1 Samuel 25 in a similar place, not with the character of Abigail herself as you might expect, but with a nation in mourning.

In verse 1, we discover that the prophet Samuel has died: "All Israel assembled and mourned for him, and they buried him in his house at Ramah."

Samuel was a man of God and the last of the Old Testament judges. He anointed Saul to be the first king of Israel, and he also anointed David to be Saul's replacement after Saul rejected God.

Of all the people who grieved when Samuel died, David probably mourned this loss as much as anyone else in Israel. Samuel had been a buffer between David and angry, violent Saul. And now Samuel is gone. David could have been feeling abandoned, vulnerable, discouraged, and wondering, *Are God's promises for my life really ever going to come true?*

Have you ever had a spiritual leader or mentor die? How did that affect you? What was your response?

In the midst of that vulnerable time in David's life, verse 1 says, "Then David rose and went down to the wilderness of Paran."

In 1 Samuel 19–24, David was fleeing for his life from King Saul. He was a fugitive. Previously he had camped out with his men in the wilderness of Engedi. After Samuel died, David moved even farther south to the wilderness of Paran to put more distance between himself and King Saul.

On the way to Paran, by the village of Carmel, David encountered a couple, of which one person loved and feared the Lord, and the other was an ungodly, selfish, wicked person.

Dive Deeper into God's Word
Read 1 Peter 3:1–4

Summarize this passage in your own words.

_____

_____

_____

_____

What is the hardest thing in this passage for you to believe and obey? Why?

_____

_____

_____

What immediate questions or thoughts do you have about this passage? Write them in the space below.

_____

_____

_____

_____

_____

Day 2: A BRIEF OVERVIEW

Read 1 Samuel 16:1–13 and 25:2–3.

Before we delve into specific verses, let's take some time to get an overview of 1 Samuel 25 and its main characters.

Give a brief description of each of the three main characters in this story. Try using words, drawings, word art, or a combination. Be creative!

NABAL

_____

_____

_____

DAVID

_____

_____

_____

ABIGAIL

_____

_____

_____

Is there a characteristic of Nabal that you see in your own life? In what circumstances are you most likely to respond like Nabal?

_____

_____

Is there a characteristic of David that you see in your own life? In what circumstances are you most likely to respond like David?

_____

_____

_____

_____

What is one characteristic of Abigail you would like God to develop in your life?

_____

_____

_____

There's also a fourth character in this story—God Himself. He is always behind the scenes ruling, overruling, and intervening in the affairs of men. He is sovereign and continually working to achieve His purposes and fulfill His promises.

What evidence of God's working do you see in this passage?

_____

_____

_____

This same God is in *your* story. How have you seen God involved with your life throughout the last week? The last month? The last year?

_____

_____

_____

_____

_____

_____

Dive Deeper into God's Word

Read 1 Peter 2:11–3:7.

This larger passage puts yesterday's verses in context. Did you notice that 3:1 starts with the word "likewise"? This word points us back to something in the previous verses. Based on today's reading, what do you think Peter is wanting us to think about as we dive into the topic of wives' submission?

_____

_____

According to this passage, who else is to be subject to authority? Which authorities does Peter mention, and what reasons does he give for the commands to be subject to them?

_____

_____

Consider the authorities you are subject to. Does this passage give you any new perspective on submitting to them when it's difficult?

_____

_____

Day 3: A BEAUTIFUL WOMAN AND A RICH MAN

Read 1 Peter 3:1–2. Reread 1 Samuel 25:2–3.

Although we've already done an overview of Nabal and Abigail's character, let's look more specifically at each of them.

How does our passage describe Nabal? If possible, look up this passage in at least three different Bible translations, and list all of the different adjectives used.

_____

_____

How is Abigail described in verses 2–3? Again, if possible, use more than one translation of the Bible.

_____

_____

Most likely, Nabal and Abigail's marriage had been arranged by her parents, as most marriages were in that culture. She probably had no say in the matter. She was beautiful; he was rich—you'd think that was a great combination. Her father may have thought he was doing her a favor by marrying her into this rich man's family. But the problem is that beauty and wealth are only external characteristics. What truly matters in real life is the heart, not outward appearance or material wealth.

In the case of this couple, the difference between their hearts could hardly have been more extreme. It was like night and day.

In Hebrew, Nabal means "fool, senseless," and Abigail means "father's joy." How do we see them live up to their names throughout this passage?

_____

_____

_____

Nabal was a foolish, ungodly man; Abigail was a wise, godly woman. We don't know if he had always been that way or had developed this character through time. All we know is that Abigail ended up in a difficult marriage.

Write out 1 Peter 3:1–2 below.

_____

_____

_____

_____

A spouse who is following Jesus and living in the power of the gospel can have a powerful influence on an ungodly mate. But **choosing to live God's way does not necessarily guarantee that your spouse (or others in your life) will be godly. Nor does it guarantee that they will change.**

Another powerful lesson we find in the story of Abigail is that **you don't have to let a harsh, badly-behaved person turn you into a harsh, badly-behaved person**. The fact that your spouse or someone else you have to be around is ungodly doesn't mean that you can't be godly yourself.

We often tend to feel that our level of godliness or spirituality is tied to the people around us. *They* make us react this way. But no one can *make* you react in an ungodly way. Your character and responses don't have to be controlled by theirs.

When you see someone acting foolishly like Nabal, how do you usually respond?

_____

_____

_____

_____

_____

Think of a person in your life who is difficult to be around. Write out a prayer, asking God to help you have Spirit-controlled responses to this person.

_____

_____

_____

_____

_____

_____

Read 1 Peter 2:18–25.

Consider Jesus and fill in the chart. What does this passage tell us that He experienced? And how did He respond?

EXPERIENCE	RESPONSE

Why did Jesus endure all of these experiences? (See vv. 21 and 24 for help.)

_____

_____

_____

Are you experiencing anything on the list above? How have you responded? If your responses are sinful, confess, believe the gospel (v. 24), and ask Jesus to help you "follow in his steps."

_____

_____

_____

Day 4: WHAT IS A FOOL?

Read Isaiah 32:6.

A key point of this study is how to deal with "Nabals," or difficult and foolish people, in your life.

What does it mean to be a fool according to Scripture? Write a short summary of what each of these verses teach about foolishness.

PSALM 14:1 _____

_____

PSALM 74:18 _____

_____

PROVERBS 1:7 _____

_____

PROVERBS 12:15 _____

_____

PROVERBS 15:5 _____

_____

PROVERBS 29:11 _____

_____

Write out your own definition of a "fool" based on the verses above.

_____

_____

When we see the word "fool" in Scripture, it's not describing someone who is *mentally* deficient, but someone who is *morally* deficient. It's a person who wants to live their life as if there was no God. A fool has no fear of God, no fear of man, and no regard for what is moral or spiritual. As a result, fools act stupidly, foolishly, and disgracefully.

As we study the examples of Nabal and Abigail, we find an important truth: **Your heart determines your behavior.** If you have a foolish heart, you will act foolishly. If you have given your heart to Jesus and you surrender to His control, then He will help you act in a way that's glorifying to the Lord.

It's easy to read about Nabal and think of someone we know. But as we go through this study, let's ask God to shine the spotlight of His Spirit and His Word into our hearts and ask ourselves, *Could any of this be true of me?* Write out your answers to the probing questions below.

- Am I sometimes impossible to deal with?

- Are people not honest with me for fear I'll blow up?

- Am I arrogant, proud, harsh?

- Do I assume the worst of others?

- Do I answer roughly rather than graciously?

The Scripture says we're all foolish from birth. Only the grace of God and the power of the gospel can transform our hearts. Apart from that, we would all be Nabals. But through God's grace, He can make us gracious, kind, and sweet-spirited in our homes and our relationships, no matter what type of people we have to deal with on a daily basis.

Read 1 Peter 3:1–6.

What words does Peter use to describe the actions and heart of a godly woman in these verses? List them out below.

_____

_____

_____

_____

From what you know of Jesus' life, how did He live out these characteristics during His life on earth?

_____

_____

_____

_____

_____

When we "follow in his steps" by living this way, God views this as "very precious" (v. 4). What emotions does this stir up in you? How does knowing that God sees your obedience in this way give you hope for dealing with difficult people?

_____

_____

_____

_____

_____

Day 5: TAKE IT HOME. MAKE IT PERSONAL

Read James 1:22.

How does having a relationship with Jesus and walking in Him keep you from being a fool?

_____

_____

What can you do this week to show grace to the foolish and difficult people in your life?

_____

_____

Write down what God taught you through the first week of this study, including any actions He wants you to take or insights He wants you to apply to your life.

_____

_____

Dive Deeper into God's Word

Read 1 Peter 3:7–22.

What are Peter's encouragements to all of us in relating to others? And what reason does he give for this (v. 9)?

_____

_____

What are the promises in this passage for those who suffer from difficult or foolish people unjustly?

_____

_____

Jesus suffered, just as we do (v. 18), but because of His suffering, we have hope! All things are subject to Him—even the ungodly authorities and foolish people we deal with (v. 22). As you move into next week, what truths from this week's passage in 1 Peter have you found to be most helpful? What practical steps will you take to apply them to your situation?

_____

_____

_____

Father, help me to live in a way that honors and glorifies You as I deal with the difficult people in my life. No matter how they treat me or if they never change, I pray that my behavior would not be controlled by their choices but by Your Holy Spirit. Lord, I also ask that You would reveal to me any marks of a fool in my own life. Forgive me for my foolishness, and help me to change. Make me kind and gracious as I interact with others—that by doing so, I would reflect Jesus Christ.

FATHER,
help me to
LIVE IN A WAY
that honors
AND GLORIFIES
you

SCRIPTURE MEMORY

Spend time meditating on and memorizing the following verse this week:

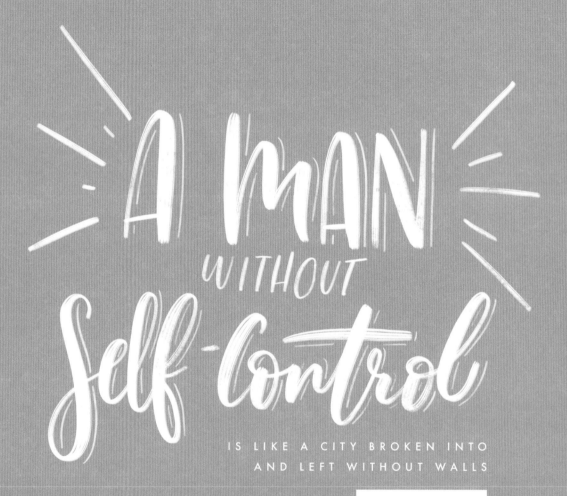

A MAN WITHOUT Self-Control IS LIKE A CITY BROKEN INTO AND LEFT WITHOUT WALLS

PROVERBS 25:28

Week 2

A REASONABLE REQUEST;
A RUDE RESPONSE

Introduction

What makes you angry during a typical day? Maybe it's an inconsiderate driver who cuts you off, a store clerk who's just downright rude, a coworker who fails to follow through on what they promised to do, or the child who disobeys for the umpteenth time. How do you respond in these kinds of situations?

In this week's study, we'll see how Nabal (who was far more inconsiderate than the average motorist, store clerk, procrastinator, or child) provoked the anger of Israel's future king. Though we may not react as extremely as David did when we are aggravated, we can be challenged to examine our responses and exercise self-control with the Lord's help.

Sheep-shearing was done in the springtime, either by the owners of the sheep (Gen. 31:19, 38:13; Deut. 15:19; 1 Sam. 25:2, 4) or by regular "shearers" (1 Sam. 25:7, 11; Isa. 53:7). In Old Testament times, there were even special houses for this work (2 Kings 10:12, 14).[3] Since sheep were chiefly valued for their wool (Deut. 18:4; Prov. 27:23, 26; 31:13; Job 31:19), the process of shearing was done extremely carefully to try and keep the fleece whole (Judg. 6:37).

Among the Hebrews, sheep shearing was a season of great festivity and parties (Gen. 31:19; 2 Samuel 13:23–28; 2 Kings 10:12, 14). In many homes, it was also a time of thanksgiving to God for the wool provided from the flocks.

Day 1: DAVID MAKES A REQUEST

Read 1 Samuel 25:4–13.

David and his 600 men were out in the wilderness when David heard that Nabal was shearing his sheep. As a herdsman himself, David surely knew that sheep-shearing wasn't just a time of work, it was also a time of feasting and festivity with friends and neighbors.

So David sent ten young men as messengers to Nabal with a request (vv. 5–8).

Write a synopsis of David's request in your own words.

_____

_____

_____

In the wilderness, David and his men treated Nabal and his herdsmen honorably. They had provided protection from thieves, bandits, and marauders for Nabal's men and herds.

Now David came back and merely asked for his rightful due: compensation for services rendered. David and his men provided protection. They made sure that marauders stayed away from Nabal's sheep and his herdsmen. Now David asked for an invitation to the feast as a reward for their service. Reasonable, right?

But Nabal's response was anything but reasonable.

> And Nabal answered David's servants, "Who is David? Who is the son of Jesse? There are many servants these days who are breaking away from their masters. Shall I take my bread and my water and my meat that I have killed for my shearers and give it to men who come from I do not know where?" (vv. 10–11).

How would you describe Nabal's response to David? What key words and phrases stand out to you?

_____

_____

_____

It's not surprising that a man who is harsh and badly behaved should speak in a way that is harsh and badly behaved.

Write down Jesus' words found in Matthew 12:34.

_____

_____

In other words, **what's in your heart comes out in the way you respond to people in your life.**

Nabal's real motives come out through his response to David's request.
What attitudes do you see Nabal's words revealing? Be as descriptive as possible.

"Who is David? Who is the son of Jesse?"

_____

_____

"There are many servants these days who are breaking away from their masters."

_____

_____

"Shall I take my bread and my water and my meat that I have killed for my shearers . . . ?"

_____

_____

"And give it to men who come from I do not know where?"

_____

_____

Nabal was a rich man. He had a lot more than he needed and could well afford to share with these men who had provided protection for him. But he refused to do so. His words were like a slap in the face to David, one of the most powerful men in the region—who was going to be the next king of Israel.

Through his response to David, we can see Nabal's obsession with his own welfare.

Look again at verse 11. How many times does Nabal use the word "my"? _____

It seems like Nabal wanted to hold on to what he had and get more, to be in control and have the upper hand over David and anyone else in his life.

While it can be easy to point the finger at Nabal, how often do we act in the same way, selfishly hanging on to "my time, my space, my stuff"? Ask God to search your heart and reveal any Nabal-like tendencies. Then, as He leads, write out a prayer of confession.

_____

_____

_____

_____

How have you seen Jesus change your heart so that it's less like Nabal and more like Him?

_____

_____

_____

_____

Dive Deeper into God's Word
Read 1 Corinthians 13.

Summarize this passage in a sentence or two. What is the main idea?

_____

_____

_____

In our study thus far, we have explored the responses of David, Nabal, and Abigail to a difficult situation. What words from 1 Corinthians 13 would you use to describe each of their behavior? Write them below.

DAVID: _____

NABAL: _____

ABIGAIL: _____

Which of the descriptions of love in this passage is the most challenging for you when dealing with difficult people? Confess this to the Lord, and ask for His grace to pursue selfless love when it's hard.

_____

_____

Day 2: DAVID'S RESPONSE

Read 1 Samuel 25:13.

As we continue in our study, we will find two very different ways to respond to the difficult people in our lives. This week, we'll look at David's response, and next week, we'll examine Abigail's.

According to verse 13, how did David react to Nabal?

_____

_____

_____

David's initial response to Nabal was to act just like Nabal—harsh, badly behaved, and contentious. He wanted vengeance, calling for 400 of his men to strap on swords as if they were going to war. This was purely an impulsive reaction; David didn't even stop to think.

Isn't that often our natural response when we're provoked? We may not strap on literal swords, but we can do as much damage with our words. Sometimes we can even retaliate by simply using our body language, our eyes, or our demeanor.

Nabal had returned evil for good to David, and now David determines to return evil for evil.

What's your natural response when you're provoked?

_____

_____

_____

_____

_____

In this case, David's response to Nabal seems to be disproportionate to the offense. Nabal had been rude, ugly, and mean, but all he'd really done was refuse to feed David and his men. This was not an offense that justified killing Nabal, all the men in his family, and all his sheepherders. David is out of control.

This type of behavior is also out of character for David, which we can see from the previous chapter.

Read 1 Samuel 24.

What did David do when he had the chance to take Saul's life? How does his response show his trust in the Lord?

_____

_____

David exercised extraordinary control in 1 Samuel 24 because he was a man after God's own heart.

But in his encounter with Nabal, it's almost as if he is caught off guard. He's out in the wilderness at a vulnerable and lonely time in his life, and he reacts impulsively to Nabal's insult.

Have you ever heard of the H.A.L.T. principle? It's something that would have served David well. The principle basically states that if you're:

- **H**ungry
- **A**ngry
- **L**onely
- **T**ired

. . . then you need to "halt," or take a moment to think before you speak or act.

At this point, David certainly had reason to be all of those things. He was hungry and responsible to feed his 600 men. He was angry; his rights had been violated. He was perhaps lonely. Samuel had died, and he may have felt abandoned. He could have easily been tired from running through the wilderness to evade Saul.

David should have halted, but instead, he let himself respond in a Nabal-like way. His resulting actions were impulsive, impetuous, and passionate. He encountered someone who was rude and insulting, and he responded in a like manner.

What guiding principles do the following verses give for when you encounter rudeness or insensitivity?

PROVERBS 26:4 _____

_____

PROVERBS 15:1 _____

_____

PROVERBS 15:18 _____

_____

JAMES 1:19-20 _____

_____

1 CORINTHIANS 13:4-5 _____

_____

Dive Deeper into God's Word
Read 1 Corinthians 13:1–3.

The Corinthians were more focused on getting prestige and attention from using certain gifts than on serving other believers sacrificially. They had forgotten that all the gifts are necessary—and all have to be used with love! What are the ways you try to stand out, look more holy, or compensate when you are in a difficult situation? Do you use your gifts to gain attention or to serve the Body of Christ (especially the people you have trouble getting along with)?

_____

_____

_____

According to these verses, what is the value of gifts used without love?

_____

_____

Rewrite this passage in your own words, replacing tongues, prophecy, etc., with the gifts and abilities you tend to value or pursue. Ask God to help you be like Paul, who considered all things as loss for the "surpassing worth of knowing Christ Jesus" (Phil. 3:8).

_____

_____

_____

_____

Day 3: RESPONDING IN SELF-CONTROL

Reread 1 Samuel 25.

David's response to Nabal demonstrated a lack of self-control, a quality mentioned over and over again in Scripture. When you have self-control, you're able to keep your emotions, impulses, and behavior under control.

What do the following verses say about self-control?

PROVERBS 25:28 _____

_____

GALATIANS 5:22–23 _____

_____

TITUS 2:11–12 _____

_____

2 PETER 1:5–7 _____

_____

Use the table below to list out the benefits of self-control and the dangers of losing control.

BENEFITS OF SELF-CONTROL	DANGERS OF LOSING CONTROL

If we don't have self-control—being able to say "yes" to what we ought to say "yes" to and say "no" to what we ought to say "no" to—then we're opening ourselves up to enemy attack.

Write out Galatians 5:22–23.

_____

_____

_____

Self-control, from a biblical standpoint, isn't about sheer willpower or human effort. It's about being under the control of the Holy Spirit in every area of your life. When we try to be self-controlled by our own power, we'll just get frustrated and fail. But when we yield to the power of the Holy Spirit, we can say "no" to our flesh and "yes" to God.

How did David's lack of self-control make him vulnerable to temptation? How has a lack of self-control done the same in your life?

In what areas of your life do you lack self-control? Write out a prayer of surrender to the power of the Holy Spirit.

_____

_____

_____

Dive Deeper into God's Word
Read 1 Corinthians 13:4–8.

Write a definition of each of the words or phrases from our passage. Use a dictionary or a Bible concordance to help.

Love . . .

Is patient. _____

Is kind. _____

Does not envy. _____

Does not boast. _____

Is not arrogant. _____

Is not rude. _____

Does not insist on its own way. _____

Is not irritable. _____

Is not resentful. _____

Does not rejoice at wrongdoing. _____

Rejoices with the truth. _____

Bears all things. _____

Believes all things. _____

Hopes all things. _____

Endures all things. _____

Never ends. _____

Do you know anyone who embodies these (or most of these) traits? How have you seen them respond in situations with people who are hard to love? How can you follow their example?

_____

_____

_____

Day 4: THE NECESSITY OF WISE COUNSEL

In David's anger and haste, he neglected to ask anyone for advice. Scripture doesn't tell us if any of David's men tried to talk him out of this decision. But we do see that they follow him as he goes to "do battle" against Nabal.

Have you ever had a trusted leader, friend, or someone close to you make an unwise decision? How did you respond?

_____

_____

_____

As we see in the example of David, even the most godly people sometimes act in ungodly, foolish ways.

Reflect on a time when you gave godly counsel to a friend who was on the edge and it made a real difference.

_____

_____

Not only do we need to be willing to *give* godly counsel, we also need to be willing to receive it. We need godly people around us to help us see when we're being foolish and who will love us enough to speak the truth.

Humility is required. True humility involves a willingness to listen to wise counsel and admit when we've been wrong.

The book of Proverbs is a wisdom book with much to say about the benefits of listening to the advice of others. Write out the benefits mentioned in the following proverbs.

PROVERBS 9:9 _____

_____

PROVERBS 11:14 _____

_____

PROVERBS 15:31-33 _____

_____

PROVERBS 28:26 _____

_____

As we continue in this study, we'll see that although David initially responded foolishly to Nabal, later on he listened to wise counsel and was willing to change his course.

Have you ever had a time when you changed your actions after receiving wise counsel? Write a brief description of the situation. What happened as a result?

_____

_____

At some point in your life, you're going to encounter people just like Nabal. But you don't have to respond like them. Even in the midst of a crisis, you can be secure, confident, godly, and courageous, letting your response glorify God.

Ultimately, you're not responsible for how others act or what they do to you. You are responsible for what you do in return. By God's grace, you can respond in a way that is faithful, appropriate, discerning, and wise. This may make all the difference in the outcome of the situation.

Dive Deeper into God's Word
Read 1 John 3:10–24 and 4:7–21.

According to these verses, who is love? What does this person do to show that love to ungodly people, and why? (See 3:16 and 4:9–10 if you need help.)

_____

_____

In verse 3:12, John gives an example of someone who responded to a difficult situation wrongly. Who is that, what did he do, and why? Have you ever been that angry at a situation, and what was your response?

_____

_____

What commands are given in this passage? List them below, and circle the ones that you are not obeying in your most difficult relationship. Confess this and ask God to forgive you, and if appropriate, go to that person and ask for their forgiveness as well. Then, rely on God's grace to obey the Truth.

_____

_____

_____

_____

Day 5: TAKE IT HOME. MAKE IT PERSONAL.

Read Titus 2:11–12.

What are some practical ways you can follow the H.A.L.T. principle this week?

_____

_____

How has the Holy Spirit helped you to practice self-control in the past? What are some ways you can tune your heart to the Spirit's voice this week in order to say "yes" to God and "no" to the flesh?

_____

_____

Write down what God has taught you through this week's study, including any actions He wants you to take or insights He wants you to apply to your life.

_____

_____

_____

_____

_____

Dive Deeper into God's Word
Read 1 Corinthians 13:4–8.

Yesterday's passage told us about the embodiment of love: Jesus Christ Himself. Match the Scriptures about Jesus to the characteristics from 1 Corinthians 13 below.

LOVE	JOHN 8:39-40, 45-46
PATIENCE	MATTHEW 20:28
KINDNESS	ROMANS 8:35-39
HUMILITY	PHILIPPIANS 2:5-8
SELFLESSNESS	HEBREWS 12:1-3
LOVE OF THE TRUTH	1 TIMOTHY 1:16
PERSEVERANCE	EPHESIANS 2:7

How has Christ personally shown His love to you when you were difficult to love? Journal about a specific time that sticks out in your memory in the space below.

_____

_____

_____

_____

_____

_____

_____

_____

_____

From this week's study in 1 Corinthians 13, what is the Holy Spirit prompting you to do to better show love to the difficult people in your life? Ask God for grace, and do it!

_____

_____

_____

_____

Father, in this world of Nabals, give me grace to be slow to anger, bring a calm spirit into tense situations, and glorify You in my response. Help me to be mindful of my own emotional and physical state so that I can stop if necessary. Lord, if I see those close to me making foolish decisions, may I speak the Truth in love. And help me to listen when others try to speak the Truth to me.

FATHER, give me GRACE TO BE slow to anger AND GLORIFY you in my RESPONSE

Spend time meditating on and memorizing the following verse this week:

the Lord will keep you from all evil; He will keep your life. The Lord will keep your going out and your coming in from this time forth and forevermore

PSALM 121:7–8

Week 3

Introduction

Imagine that you have just received some bad news about your family's finances. How are you likely to respond? Would you ignore the problem and block it out of your mind? Launch a tirade of complaints to anyone who will listen? Become overwhelmed by fear or depression? Or pray about it and then take the necessary action through God's power?

Our responses are an overflow of the condition of our hearts (Luke 6:45). When we find our security in the One who holds our hearts, the Lord changes how we handle our circumstances. In our study this week, we'll look at how Abigail responded when she received potentially devastating news for herself and her whole family.

Submission does not mean that:

- Men are superior to women.

- Women can't express their opinions or give input.

- Men are always right.

- Women should overlook sin in the lives of those in authority.

- Women who are being abused should not seek help from pastors or authorities.

- Women are to be submissive to all men. Rather they are to be submissive only to the men God has placed in authority over them.

- Those in authority have a license to be abusive, domineering, or disrespectful of those under their authority.

Day 1: A WISE AND DISCERNING WOMAN

Read 1 Samuel 25:14–31.

Write a short synopsis of this passage. Circle key words and phrases.

_____

_____

_____

Why would one of Nabal's young men go to Abigail to report what happened between Nabal and David?

_____

_____

_____

In verses 14–17, how did the messenger describe David's treatment of Nabal's men? How did he describe Nabal and his reaction?

_____

_____

_____

Abigail was caught between two proud, angry men—Nabal (her husband) and David, the future king of Israel. Abigail stood in contrast. She responded differently to Nabal than David did. *She didn't become foolish as she responded to the fool in her life.*

Revisit 1 Samuel 25:3. How is Abigail's character described?

_____

_____

What does the way Abigail handled this crisis reveal about her heart?

_____

_____

The word *discerning* means "showing good or outstanding judgment or understanding" or "intelligent." A discerning woman has good understanding and common sense in a crisis.

Who do you know that is a discerning woman?

_____

_____

Abigail saw the brewing conflict between her husband and David, who were both acting like fools. She used discernment and chose to respond differently.

Use the chart below to record Abigail's actions (and inactions).

WHAT DID ABIGAIL DO IN RESPONSE TO THIS CRISIS?	WHAT DID ABIGAIL NOT DO?

Did any of these observations make your lists?

- **Abigail didn't cower in fear.** Even though she probably had fear in her heart, she didn't let it keep her from doing the wise and right thing.

- **Abigail listened to the warning of her husband's employee**, unlike Nabal, who wouldn't listen to anyone.

- **Abigail didn't sit back and do nothing.** She wasn't passive. Instead, **she took action.** She moved quickly, wisely, calmly, and decisively. She was organized and prepared for an emergency. A woman who walks with God will be prepared to act wisely in a crisis. But don't expect that once you get in the crisis you can take a crash course and become a wise woman overnight. If you've not been already growing in wisdom and discernment, you'll easily be caught off guard and without direction in a crisis situation.

Abigail also showed wisdom in knowing **when to speak and when not to speak.** After describing all the ways that Abigail prepared to defuse this crisis, Scripture says, "But she did not tell her husband Nabal" (v. 19). She likely knew at that moment Nabal was in no frame of mind to listen, so she wisely refrained from saying anything to him *at that time.*

Abigail knew **to whom she should speak.** She knew that David had a heart for God, and she likely determined that he could be reasoned with.

How did Abigail demonstrate the following attributes in her response to the situation?

COURAGE _____

_____

HUMILITY _____

_____

COMPOSURE _____

_____

RESPECT _____

_____

CONTROL _____

_____

CLARITY _____

_____

DIGNITY _____

_____

SINCERITY _____

_____

What characteristics of Christ do you see demonstrated by Abigail?

_____

_____

Are you facing any crisis situations today—big or small? In what ways can you follow Abigail's example in your response?

_____

_____

Dive Deeper into God's Word
Read Psalm 121.

At the very beginning of this psalm, it says this is "a song of ascents," a psalm that the Israelites would sing as they traveled to visit the temple at Jerusalem. They would walk up the mountain (or "hills") the city was built on and sing to remember who God is. Do you sing any specific songs to "lift up" your eyes to God? If so, what attributes of God or truths do they focus on? Do these songs have anything in common with this psalm?

_____

_____

_____

The temple was a physical reminder to the Israelites of God's presence that they could look at, touch, and experience. Do you have any similar reminders in your life—things that point your heart to Christ through hearing, taste, touch, smell, or sight? If not, is there anything you could add to your home or workspace that could serve as such a reminder?

_____

_____

Make a list of the words or phrases in this psalm that describe the Lord and what He does. We'll dig deeper into some of these descriptions the rest of this week.

_____

_____

Day 2: WAS ABIGAIL SUBMISSIVE?

Read Ephesians 5:22–24.

Abigail did not make excuses for her husband. She was honest about the offense, but she did so in a respectful way. It seems that her goal was not to tear her husband down or to get somebody on her side, but rather to insert the voice of wisdom and reason into a tense situation.

Perhaps as you've read Abigail's story, you've wondered whether or not she was being submissive to her husband. After all, didn't she go behind his back by giving food to David? Wasn't she showing a lack of respect for her husband in the way she spoke about him?

Let's examine the bigger picture of submission.

God has established order, headship, authority, and submission in every sphere of life—in the home, in the church, in the workplace, in the government. Submission is not just for women. Submission is also for men. Submission is for young, old, married, and single. Everyone has to submit to one or more human authorities in their lives, and all of us are to submit to God's ultimate sovereign authority.

Use the chart below to record what God's Word teaches about submission.

INSTRUCTIONS FOR ALL CHRISTIANS	INSTRUCTIONS FOR CHRISTIAN WIVES
JAMES 4:7 _____	COLOSSIANS 3:18 _____
_____	_____
EPHESIANS 5:21 _____	EPHESIANS 5:22-24 _____
_____	_____
1 PETER 2:13-14 _____	1 PETER 3:1-2 _____
_____	_____
HEBREWS 13:17 _____	1 PETER 3:5-6 _____
_____	_____

In marriage and in the church, the responsibility for leadership (or headship) is given by God to men. Men are responsible to lead, protect, and provide for the women under their care and to exercise that leadership in a way that is loving, humble, and servant-hearted. Our responsibility as women is to respond to that leadership in humility, graciously following and submitting to God-ordained authority. That does not mean we are to be brainless or weak or spineless. In fact, it takes incredible wisdom and strength of character to submit well, following the biblical pattern for submission.

Write your own definition of submission. Has your view of submission changed since you first became a Christian? If so, how?

_____

_____

As we consider this question of whether or not Abigail was submissive to her husband, let's keep in mind that Abigail did not have the advantage that we have of the New Testament's teaching, so she was not necessarily a perfect example of how women in a New Testament sense should act.

Based on what we've discussed above, do you think Abigail was being submissive? Why or why not?

_____

_____

Dive Deeper into God's Word
Read Psalm 121:1–2 and Job 38–39.

How does Psalm 121:2 describe the God who is the source of your help?

_____

_____

What description in the Job passage about God's power, sovereignty, or wisdom is most difficult for you to fathom? What gives you the most comfort?

_____

_____

_____

Based on these two readings, write a prayer or draw a response to God's revelation of Himself as the all-powerful Creator who sends help.

_____

_____

_____

Day 3: LOOKING AT THE BIG PICTURE, PART 1

Read 1 Samuel 25:28–29.

As Abigail spoke to David, she respectfully called him "my lord." And then she brought the Lord into the picture. She knew that David, unlike her husband, had a heart for God, so she appealed to David to see this situation from God's point of view.

Look again at 1 Samuel 25:28–29. Circle any mention of "the Lord." Underline any mention of "lord."

> "For the Lord will certainly make my lord a sure house, because my lord is fighting the battles of the Lord, and evil shall not be found in you so long as you live. If men rise up to pursue you and to seek your life, the life of my lord shall be bound in the bundle of the living in the care of the Lord your God. And the lives of your enemies he shall sling out as from the hollow of a sling." (vv. 28–29)

According to verse 29, what would happen to David if he continued to trust God?

_____

What would happen to the unrighteous enemies of David?

_____

Abigail challenged David to look at the big picture of God's plan and to not return evil for evil. She affirmed him in fighting the Lord's battle. And she reminded David of God's protection and care for those who belong to the Lord, and of the judgment that awaits those who oppose God and His servants.

In what ways do you see these themes throughout the whole Word of God?

_____

_____

Record Abigail's words from verse 29.

_____

_____

That phrase "bound in the bundle of the living" refers to the practice of taking your valuables and wrapping them up in a bundle to keep them safe. If you are a child of God, that verse describes your position in Christ. Your life is bundled in the care of the Lord, under the protection of divine Providence. He has put you into a special place and wrapped you up in Christ, where you are safe.

How do these passages assure you of God's care and protection?

2 SAMUEL 22:3-4 _____

_____

ISAIAH 41:10 _____

_____

JOHN 10:28-30 _____

_____

Abigail was a woman who knew what it was like—from living in this difficult marriage—to have her life bundled up in the life of the Lord her God. She couldn't escape her difficult circumstances, but she knew that her inner person was safe. She could confidently say to David, "No matter what Nabals come into your life, your life is bundled up in the life of the Lord your God."

If you are a child of God, then you are bundled up in His eternal protection. No matter what temporary trouble you face, you can rest knowing He will protect you forever. Nothing can hurt or harm you that He cannot deliver you in or through or out of. He is watching over you in every detail of your life.

What mental picture comes to mind when you consider being "bundled up" in God's love? Describe it or draw a picture below.

_____

_____

_____

_____

How does knowing that you're bundled up in Christ's eternal protection encourage you?

_____

_____

Dive Deeper into God's Word
Read Psalm 121 and Exodus 3:1–4:17.

Have you noticed the name of God that is used in Psalm 121? Depending on your translation, it likely says "Lord" (in all caps or small caps). That's how we render God's personal name, Yahweh (or I am who I am) into English.

Look up "Yahweh" in a Bible dictionary and write down some of what it means below.

_____

_____

When God called Moses into an impossible situation, dealing with impossible people—Pharaoh and the Egyptians, and the Israelites themselves—He revealed Himself as Yahweh, the I AM, and promised to be with Moses, give him words to speak, and bring deliverance. What do you need in your situation? Words? Promises to hold you fast? God's presence? Something to change? Write or speak a prayer to Yahweh, asking Him to provide what you need in dealing with difficult people.

_____

_____

_____

_____

_____

_____

How does having Yahweh as your helper give you hope today? Write about it here, and share that hope with a friend or your study group.

_____

_____

Day 4: LOOKING AT THE BIG PICTURE, PART 2

Read Revelation 6:10.

Abigail not only reminded David of the Lord's protection, she also emphasized that God's enemies will face His righteous judgment and they will be removed from His presence like a stone being shot from a sling. It's a good reminder for us as well. Consider the following truths.

First, if we don't know Christ as our Savior, then we all deserve to be "slung out" because of our sins.

Read Psalm 14:3, Romans 3:23, and Ephesians 2:1–3. What do these passages teach us?

_____

_____

Jesus made a way for us to escape God's judgment, if we trust Him as our Savior. Read John 3:16; and Romans 5:8, 10:9–10. What do these passages teach us?

_____

_____

God will deal with the Nabals in this world. Whether you're married to one, the neighbor of one, the employee of one, or even in the same church as one, there will come a day when they will face the judgment of God.

Write out Proverbs 11:21 below.

_____

_____

_____

_____

How does knowing that God will deal with the Nabals in the world help you as you face insults, false accusations, and injustice?

_____

_____

You may be facing a situation with a Nabal today that seems like it will never end. Maybe you've been married to an unbelieving spouse for decades. Maybe you're in a job with an unreasonable and harsh boss and you just want to get out, but God hasn't opened any other doors for employment. Maybe your next-door neighbor is making your life miserable, and you can't even feel peace in your own backyard.

Your heart is crying out, "God, when? When will You take care of this situation? When will You exact Your justice?" Isn't that what we hear in the book of Revelation as those in heaven cry out and say, "O Sovereign Lord, holy and true, how long before you will judge and avenge our blood on those who dwell on the earth" (6:10)?

Write out your own version of this verse as a prayer below.

_____

_____

_____

_____

_____

We don't know how long it will be until God brings justice. But we know that in God's way and His time, He will sling out, discard, and destroy all those who are evildoers. In the meantime, you can rest assured that your life is "bound in the bundle of the living in the care of the Lord your God."

Dive Deeper into God's Word
Read Psalm 121.

All throughout this psalm, we learn that God is our keeper. (Your translation may have the words "protect," "preserve," or "watch" instead.) Take a close look: how many times does this idea or word appear? _____

According to this psalm, what does God keep? And what does He keep you from? Make a list below.

_____

_____

What do you need Yahweh to keep or keep you from? Rewrite this psalm in your own words, as a personal prayer to Him, inserting your specific needs and fears.

_____

_____

_____

_____

_____

_____

_____

_____

Day 5: TAKE IT HOME. MAKE IT PERSONAL.

Read 2 Timothy 1:14.

How can you guard against becoming a Nabal in your interactions with your family? With your employer and coworkers? With your neighbors, friends, and people at church?

_____

_____

_____

_____

Take some time today and creatively thank God for "bundling you up" in Jesus. Sing a worship song, write a poem, paint a picture, or do something else. Afterward, write below how your chosen activity helped you to put your focus on God rather than your circumstances.

_____

_____

Dive Deeper into God's Word
Read Psalm 121:3–7.

Shaky ground, night, evil, death . . . the psalmist is honest about his fears. As you've studied Abigail's life and how God helps you deal with difficult people, have you been honest with Him about your fears about your situation? Take time now to list them out below in the first column.

Now, using the second column, write who God is or what He does in the face of each fear. In the box at the bottom of the chart, summarize all this truth about God in one sentence. Then put this sentence somewhere that it can remind you often about how Yahweh, the watchful Creator, keeps you "from all evil" as you deal with difficult people.

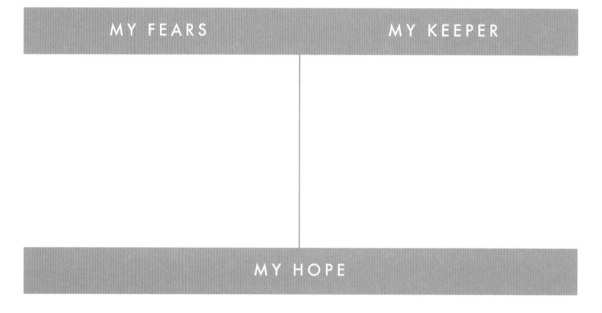

MY FEARS   MY KEEPER

MY HOPE

Lord, in times of crisis, I want to be a voice of reason and respond with a wise and discerning spirit. Help me to develop those qualities in times of peace, so that when the hard times come I will be ready. Remind me each day to keep the big picture of Your plan in mind. Even when it seems that difficult situations will never change and that those who are against me will never see justice, help me to rest in Your promise that my life is bound up in the bundle of Your care.

LORD, help me to REST IN YOUR promise that my LIFE IS BOUND UP in the bundle OF YOUR CARE

Spend time meditating on and memorizing the following verse this week:

the SALVATION OF THE righteous is FROM the LORD

HE IS THEIR STRONGHOLD IN THE TIME OF TROUBLE.
THE LORD HELPS THEM AND DELIVERS THEM;
HE DELIVERS THEM FROM THE WICKED AND SAVES
THEM, BECAUSE THEY TAKE REFUGE IN HIM

PSALM 37:39-40

Week 4

Introduction

It reads like a scene straight out of a blockbuster movie.

The handsome hero is on the run from a powerful and jealous man. Unjustly accused, he and a group of his loyal friends are simply trying to survive. Then the hero stops to help out a local businessman and in return gets stabbed in the back.

Enraged, the hero calls his friends to help him fight back and get satisfaction against this man who has insulted him and treated him so poorly . . .

Be Still, My Soul

By Katharina von Schlegel (1697–1797), trans. Jane Borthwick

Be still, my soul: the Lord is on your side;
bear patiently the cross of grief or pain;
leave to your God to order and provide;
in ev'ry change he faithful will remain.
Be still, my soul: your best, your heav'nly Friend
through thorny ways leads to a joyful end.

Be still, my soul: your God will undertake
to guide the future as he has the past.
Your hope, your confidence let nothing shake;
all now mysterious shall be bright at last.
Be still, my soul: the waves and winds still know
his voice who ruled them while he dwelt below.

Be still, my soul: when dearest friends depart,
and all is darkened in the vale of tears,
then shall you better know his love, his heart,
who comes to soothe your sorrow and your fears.
Be still, my soul: your Jesus can repay
from his own fullness all he takes away.

Be still, my soul: the hour is hast'ning on
when we shall be forever with the Lord,
when disappointment, grief, and fear are gone,
sorrow forgot, love's purest joys restored.
Be still, my soul: when change and tears are past,
all safe and blessed we shall meet at last.

If this story was in a movie theater, we would expect the hero to take revenge on his enemies as the audience cheered. That's because the world considers vengeance to be a virtue. But in God's economy, things are different. Rather than seek vengeance ourselves, we are to recognize that it belongs to the Lord.

In the story that God has written, how will our hero, who is bent on revenge, respond when he's reminded of this truth? Let's find out.

Day 1: LEAVE THE REVENGE TO GOD

Read 1 Samuel 25:30–38.

In our study last week, Abigail went before David to appeal for the lives of her husband and her household. She showed great wisdom and discretion in how she responded to Nabal and the way she urged David to look at the big picture of God's care and sovereignty.

Now, we come to the final words of her appeal. Read verses 30–31 again.

Summarize Abigail's request to David in your own words.

_____

_____

_____

Why did Abigail urge David to let God deal with Nabal rather than taking revenge?

_____

_____

_____

Earlier in her appeal to David, Abigail said something similar: "Now then, my lord, as the Lord lives, and as your soul lives, because the Lord has restrained you from bloodguilt and from saving with your own hand" (v. 26). These words, "saving with your own hand," is a reference to getting vengeance or avenging yourself—basically taking matters into your own hands. Abigail warned that David needed to stop and let God deal with it.

That's a concept we see clearly spelled out in the New Testament. Record what Romans 12:17–18 teaches.

_____

_____

Sometimes people won't respond to your best efforts to live peaceably with them, as Nabal didn't respond well to David. David sent his men and said, "Peace be to you," and Nabal essentially said, "Too bad, I'm not interested in peace."

So what do you do when people won't live peaceably with you? Proverbs 20:22 gives us a clear, practical step to take. Write out this verse below.

_____

_____

_____

The following verses offer more insight. Look them up, and next to the references below, summarize the action step we are encouraged to take. (Or not take.)

ROMANS 12:19-21 _____

_____

1 THESSALONIANS 5:15 _____

_____

_____

What's the bottom line of what these passages are teaching?

_____

_____

Dive Deeper into God's Word

Read Romans 12:9–21.

In this passage, we're given a list of imperatives (or commands) on how to deal with people. How specifically are we commanded to handle those who mistreat us?

_____

_____

_____

Have you ever taken things into your own hands when you were mistreated? How about a time that you chose to leave vengeance to the Lord? What were the results of each situation?

_____

_____

_____

Verse 19 gives us a promise from the Lord. What is it? Are you in a situation where this truth is difficult to believe? What would change if you fully believed this promise to be true?

_____

_____

_____

Day 2: DAVID'S RESPONSE

Read 1 Samuel 25:32–35.

When David learned of Nabal's insult, his immediate reaction was to put on his sword and call his 400 men to do the same. Then there came Nabal's wife before this army, interceding for her foolish husband.

Summarize David's response.

_____

_____

_____

What does David's response show about his character?

_____

_____

What parts of Abigail's character did David praise?

_____

_____

In 1 Samuel 25:3, Abigail is described as "discerning and beautiful." It was her discernment, not just her beauty, that David found attractive in this situation.

When Abigail confronted David, she did it graciously, clearly, and directly. She spoke the truth, but she did so respectfully and humbly. She was not strident, contentious, domineering, or controlling like her husband. Through her example, we learn that you can say hard things to even the most difficult of people when you say them with a gentle and gracious spirit, genuine concern, and compassion.

Proverbs 11:22 gives a graphic word picture of the woman who has natural physical beauty but doesn't have internal discretion and good judgment. Write it out below or draw a picture to represent the verse.

_____

_____

_____

Ultimately your greatest impact won't be made by your outward appearance. It will be through your heart, attitude, and words.

Abigail was the key to defuse this volatile situation. She couldn't control her husband. She couldn't control David. But she could control herself, and by being wise with what she said and how she said it, she was able to convince David to change directions.

How is effective speech described in the following verses?

PROVERBS 15:1 _____

_____

PROVERBS 16:21 _____

_____

PROVERBS 16:32 _____

_____

PROVERBS 25:15 _____

_____

In a crisis, harsh and controlling words come out naturally for most of us. But Abigail didn't go there, and as a result, her soft answer turned away David's wrath.

In what situations are you most tempted to speak harshly?

_____

_____

Lives were spared through Abigail's wise handling of the situation. She was able to get David's eyes off himself and his enemies and onto the Lord.

Dive Deeper into God's Word
Read Isaiah 53.

What does Isaiah 53 tell us about how Jesus was mistreated?

_____

_____

_____

Why did He suffer these things? (Check out vv. 4–6, 8 for the answer.)

_____

_____

_____

How did Jesus respond to the action of sinful, foolish people (like us) against Him?

_____

_____

_____

Day 3: A TIME TO SPEAK

Read 1 Samuel 25:36.

Ecclesiastes 3:7 tells us there is "a time to keep silence, and a time to speak." Abigail wisely practiced this concept when she returned home.

Nabal, who had refused to give food, drink, or any sustenance to David and his men, was eating and drinking as if he were a king. This arrogant, self-centered, gluttonous man thought he was more worthy of a feast than David, who would actually *be* king one day.

Why was it wise for Abigail to choose not to bring up big issues with her husband at this instance? What factors could have impeded conversation between her and Nabal?

_____

_____

_____

When did Abigail choose to tell her husband? What was the result?

_____

_____

Abigail took action once it was a good time to speak. God took action, too.

What events do verses 37 and 38 record?

_____

_____

_____

_____

We don't know for sure what happened, but apparently, Nabal had some sort of stroke or heart attack, which left him paralyzed or comatose until he died ten days later. Was it the shock? Was it the alcohol? Was it the partying lifestyle? We don't know. What we do know is that God is the one who took his life. How can we know?

_____

_____

What answer does Job 14:5 reveal?

_____

_____

_____

This isn't a fairytale ending. Scripture doesn't tell us whether Abigail had longed and prayed for her husband to become a godly man. Perhaps she had. She was a godly woman and probably wanted to see her husband change. He never did.

It's possible that one or more of the Nabals in your own life may never change or repent. You can't control that. But in the midst of that situation, you can seek to be the woman God wants you to be.

How can you live out your faith in Christ as you deal with the difficult people in your life?

_____

_____

_____

How does this passage help you in praying for the Nabals in your own life?

_____

_____

_____

Read Romans 12:9–21 and Isaiah 53.

Compare these two passages. Based on Isaiah 53, what specific imperatives from Romans 12 do you see Him living out?

_____

_____

_____

He's not just our model. Because of His death and resurrection, Jesus makes our obedience to Romans 12 possible. This is the promise of the gospel (the good news of Jesus)! How would you explain the gospel to someone else in a difficult situation? (If you're unsure, reading the entire book of Romans can give you a solid starting place.)

_____

_____

_____

_____

Find a creative way to thank the Lord Jesus for His suffering on your behalf. You could give a gift to a person or ministry that has helped you, write a song, create a sculpture, or even dance with joy! Use the abilities He's given you to praise Him, even though circumstances right now may be difficult. Write what you did below.

_____

_____

_____

_____

_____

Day 4: HE WILL DELIVER YOU

Read Psalm 37.

Maybe you've been working on this study of Abigail with a heavy heart. You're growing in the qualities that Abigail demonstrated. You've tried to be a peacemaker and have used your words to defuse dangerous situations. But your Nabal still has not changed.

God isn't surprised by your situation, and He offers hope and an invitation to take refuge in Him.

Read Psalm 37 again, slowly and carefully.

How will God ultimately reward the righteous?

_____

_____

_____

How will He judge the wicked?

_____

_____

How are we to respond to the wicked in the meantime?

_____

_____

How do the promises in this psalm give you hope in your own situation?

_____

_____

Ultimately, God delivered Abigail out of her difficult situation, and God promises that in His way and in His time, He will deliver you, too, though it may not be until Jesus returns or you go home to be with Him.

That doesn't mean you just sit by and let your husband destroy himself and your family, or your bitter sibling to continue to cause family division, or your rude co-worker to keep cutting you down. Abigail didn't sit at home and wait for David and Nabal to destroy each other.

We're not always called to sit back passively. Instead, we're to cry out to the Lord while we exercise discretion and use wisdom. We can go to people who can possibly be a part of the solution, with the goal to reconcile and redeem the situation—to see the Nabals in your life brought to repentance.

Nabal's life is a serious warning. When God determines we've reached the limit, our lives will be over, just as it was with Nabal. *Now* is the time to repent and receive Christ's forgiveness and promise of new life and to treat others with grace and dignity. Don't wait! We never know when the end will come.

Abigail's life provides a word to wise women: **Your life has influence and power if you are filled with the Spirit and Word of God. Wait on the Lord.** Don't take matters into your own hands. Act wisely, courageously, and decisively to do what you need to do in the situation. No matter how out of control things may seem, it's never out of God's control. You can take refuge in Him.

Dive Deeper into God's Word
Read Romans 12:9–21.

As you read this passage, circle any specific commands given. Pray through these verses, asking the Holy Spirit to reveal areas you are not obeying.

Day 5: TAKE IT HOME. MAKE IT PERSONAL.

Read Romans 12:17–18.

Is there a person in your life with whom you need to make an effort to live peaceably? What action could you take this week to move toward peace with them?

_____

_____

_____

Spend time praying for the Nabals in your life who need to repent and believe that Jesus is their Savior. Write out your prayer for them below.

_____

_____

_____

_____

_____

Write down what God has taught you through this week's study, including any actions He wants you to take or insights He wants you to apply to your life.

_____

_____

_____

_____

_____

Dive Deeper into God's Word
Read Romans 12:9–21 and Psalm 37.

Our Romans passage is all about peacemaking. In what relationship is it most difficult for you to live at peace (v. 18)? Write an honest prayer to the Lord about it. Tell Him the pain, and don't shy away from any difficult feelings you have.

_____

_____

_____

_____

_____

_____

Did any of what you wrote surprise you? Now take it to the Lord. Ask Him to avenge you, either through judgment or through taking it upon Himself and bringing salvation to that person. Also, ask Him to help you remember the cost of your own sin and give you the ability to respond with His heart to that person who wronged you.

_____

_____

_____

Psalm 37, where our memory verse comes from, is full of promises you can take with you as you wait for God to bring peace. Write the one that is most precious to you below.

_____

_____

_____

Father, thank You that I can trust You to take care of the difficult people in my life. When I'm tempted to take matters into my own hands, may I let You deal with it instead. During those times—and at all times and with all people—help me to have a gentle and gracious spirit that is under Your control. Give me wisdom to know when to speak and when to stay silent. Teach me to exercise discretion in my words and my actions. Thank You that my life is never out of Your control.

FATHER, thank you THAT MY LIFE is never out OF YOUR CONTROL

SCRIPTURE MEMORY

Spend time meditating on and memorizing the following verse this week:

FOR THIS LIGHT MOMENTARY AFFLICTION IS PREPARING FOR US AN ETERNAL WEIGHT OF GLORY BEYOND ALL COMPARISON, AS WE LOOK NOT TO THE THINGS THAT ARE SEEN BUT TO THE THINGS THAT ARE UNSEEN. FOR THE THINGS THAT ARE SEEN ARE TRANSIENT, BUT

the Things that are Unseen are Eternal

2 CORINTHIANS 4:17–18

Week 5

Introduction

Our fleshly nature is quick to tell us what is best: where we need to live, who we need to marry, when we are treated poorly and deserve justice, or what we need for a happy ending. Followers of Jesus already have the happiest ending, but it's easy to lose sight of the glory that's coming. Fueled by our desire for control, we tend to act from our limited perspectives which lead to foolishness, discontentment, and hopelessness.

This week we'll see how God saved David from making a mistake that would've been detrimental had he handled the situation instinctively. God demonstrates His trustworthiness in this story, reminding us that He will one day deliver us and bring all unrighteousness to an end. We'll also see how keeping eternity at the front of our minds causes us to be like Abigail—being the women God calls us to be, fully surrendered to Him.

The imprecatory psalms are those that call for God to pour out His wrath on the psalmist's enemies or those who are the enemies of God.[6] The verb "imprecate" means to invoke or call down (evil or curses), as upon a person, which is where these prayers got their name. The imprecatory psalms include Psalm 5, 10, 11, 17, 35, 55, 58, 59, 69, 70, 79, 83, 109, 129, 137, and 140.[7]

Day 1: THE LORD WILL AVENGE

Read 1 Samuel 25:39–42.

When we finished our study last week, Nabal had just dropped dead. Can you imagine being David and hearing this news? He had certainly wanted to kill Nabal and even tried before Abigail interceded for her husband.

What was David's response to the news of Nabal's death?

_____

_____

_____

What did he specifically thank God for?

_____

_____

Through this experience, David learned an important lesson: to let the Lord avenge the insults he received. In fact, David would need this lesson in the very next chapter of 1 Samuel, when he faced another Nabal in his life—King Saul.

Read 1 Samuel 26:7–12.

What happened during David's encounter with Saul in this passage? How did David show that he trusted God to take care of Saul?

_____

_____

_____

Even though David had the chance to take Saul's life, he chose to trust that in God's time and way, evil would be avenged. In Nabal's case, this happened fairly quickly. With Saul, it didn't happen for years.

God may not bring judgment on the Nabals in your life quickly. It may not even happen in your lifetime. But He will do it.

Write out Proverbs 29:23.

_____

_____

_____

How do you see this truth illustrated in Nabal's life?

_____

_____

_____

How you do you see this truth illustrated in David's life?

_____

_____

_____

David humbled himself in his response to Abigail's appeal. He chose to let go of his pride and let God deal with the person who had wronged him.

What's keeping you from trusting God today to avenge evil in your life?

_____

_____

Dive Deeper into God's Word
Read 2 Corinthians 4:6–18.

Summarize this passage in your own words. What is the main idea?

_____

_____

_____

According to this passage, what is the "treasure" God has given us?

_____

_____

_____

What do you think Paul means by "jars of clay" (v. 7)? How does having this treasure in jars of clay bring God glory?

_____

_____

_____

Day 2: PRAYING FOR GOD'S JUDGMENT, PART 1

Read Psalm 10.

Trusting God to avenge evil doesn't mean we ask God to kill the Nabals in our life. Our main request should be for God to bring them to repentance.

But this brings up a question. Is it ever right for us to just honestly say to the Lord, "I wish You would judge this person"?

If not, why does it seem like that kind of prayer is mentioned so many times in the psalms?

_____

_____

_____

We find one such example in Psalm 10. What sort of situation do the first eleven verses of Psalm 10 describe?

_____

_____

How did the psalmist ask God to handle the situation in verses 12–15?

_____

_____

Can you think of a time when you felt like praying for God's judgment on a wicked person?

_____

_____

_____

Psalm 10 is what commentators call an imprecatory psalm—a call for God to bring His judgment down on evildoers. Before we pray the same, we need to first consider our heart motives and ask ourselves our reasons for wanting God to avenge the wicked.

- Do we want God's judgment so we can be in a happier circumstance and situation? Is our goal to be released and relieved of the pressure?

- Or is our ultimate goal that God would be vindicated—that people would see Him as the just Judge and God that He is so they would turn and worship Him?

As an example, when we see reports of terrorist activity on the news, how should we pray for terrorists? It's certainly right to pray for God to save them. The Bible says that God doesn't want anyone to perish but longs for *all* people to be brought to repentance (2 Peter 3:9). But there also comes a time when we can pray, "Lord, punish evildoers for Your glory, so people can know that You are not a God to be trifled with."

If God never judged the wicked, what would the world be like? How would people view God?

_____

_____

Dive Deeper into God's Word
Read 2 Corinthians 4:6–18.

Circle the words that describe how you feel about your current circumstances.

AFFLICTED	DESPAIRING	STRUCK DOWN
CRUSHED	PERSECUTED	DESTROYED
PERPLEXED	FORSAKEN	CARRYING JESUS' DEATH

Paul gives several reasons for the suffering we deal with. List as many as you can find below. (Hint: look for the words "to," "so that," and "for.")

_____

_____

_____

Do you often "lose heart" (v. 16)? If so, which of these reasons gives you the most comfort in your situation?

_____

_____

Day 3: PRAYING FOR GOD'S JUDGMENT, PART 2

Read Revelation 16:7.

We don't wish the judgment of God on anyone, but if we love His glory and His holiness, then we need to honor Him as a God of justice who judges appropriately. We desire for Him to be glorified in the lives of all people, and for those who continue to be unrepentant, sometimes that happens through His judgment.

Before we pray that kind of prayer, we need to search our own hearts. Don't ask God to judge someone else for something that *you* deserve judgment for yourself. Pray very carefully with the glory of God in mind.

Sometimes, if someone has really hurt us, we don't want them to repent. Truth be told, we may want to see them suffer because they've made us suffer. That's where we need to be honest and confess our sinful heart attitudes to the Lord.

Spend some time interceding for the Nabals in your life. As you do, keep the following points in mind.

- Examine your own heart. Take a few minutes to ask God to reveal any sinful actions or attitudes you have allowed into your life.

- Be honest with God about the way you feel, without justifying your own hatred or hurt feelings. Cry out to God about any tough relationships you're in right now and ask for His perspective.

- Pray for those who are causing you the most hurt. Ask God to save them in His mercy and to do whatever it takes to bring that person to repentance.

Read 2 Corinthians 4:13–18.

Paul gives us an eternal perspective by pointing us to the resurrection and to the coming glory. How does the resurrection give you hope in your circumstances?

_____

_____

_____

_____

In Paul's suffering, he saw grace extending "to more and more people." How have you seen your suffering (with difficult people or otherwise) bring grace to others? Or how have you seen this happen through others' lives?

_____

_____

_____

Verse 16 talks about "our inner self . . . being renewed day by day." What are some practical ways that God renews your inner self? And what truths from Scripture bring you renewed life and hope in suffering? Write them below.

_____

_____

_____

_____

_____

Day 4: A HAPPY ENDING?

Read 1 Samuel 25:39–44.

We all like stories with a happy ending. For years, Hollywood has been teaching us that every problem can be solved and every question can be answered. For believers in Christ, there is an ultimate happy ending waiting at the end of this life. But our problems will never fully go away this side of heaven.

The conclusion of Abigail's story seems like a Hollywood ending. But was it?

_____

_____

What elements of a traditional happy ending do you find in this passage?

_____

_____

What tells you that Abigail's problems still may not be entirely over?

_____

_____

From this snapshot alone, Abigail's life looks like a fairytale, but even after marrying David, things weren't perfect. For one thing, David had multiple wives. She also had to wander in the wilderness with him and his band of 600 men as a fugitive for several years. And then years later, in unbridled passion, her husband committed adultery with Bathsheba. Heartache was not yet over in this woman's life.

It can be tempting to fantasize about circumstances that we think would put a happy ending on our own story. It is easy to start thinking, *If only . . .*

If only I had a new house . . .
If only I had a husband . . .
If only I had a different boss . . .
If only I had a more reliable car . . .
If only I wasn't stuck in this town . . .
If only my husband would take more initiative . . .
If only I had more education and could get a new job . . .
If only my husband would die. Then I could marry so and so . . .

. . . then I would be happy.

In reality, every situation and circumstance of life has its challenges.

What circumstances or desires tempt you to be discontented?

_____

_____

_____

How can the following verses help you when you're tempted to play the "if only" game?

1 TIMOTHY 6:6-8 _____

_____

PHILIPPIANS 4:11-12 _____

_____

Followers of Christ can be content in every circumstance because we know there is a true happy ending coming. There's no trouble-free existence this side of heaven, but God is good. He is in the process of sanctifying and redeeming this fallen creation, and that includes you.

Those who are righteous will live "happily ever after." But the happy ending is not here. It's not now. That's why we have to take the long view, which really isn't so long when we see it in the light of eternity.

Write a summary of how the following verses help us to have a long-term view.

2 CORINTHIANS 4:17-18 _____

_____

1 PETER 5:10 _____

_____

If you find yourself struggling with a Nabal in your life, don't lose hope. Cling to God's promises. Look ahead to the end of the story and know that in God's way and time, He will avenge all evil. He will bless and reward you if He is your refuge.

While you wait for the happily ever after, what do you do?
You wait on the Lord.
You learn wisdom.
At times, you endure hardship and suffering.*
You let God use your life to influence the Davids and the Nabals, since you don't yet know who will be an unresponsive Nabal and who will be responsive like David.

What else can you do to wait well? Add to the list above.

_____

_____

*This does not mean that if you are in a physically abusive situation you should just endure it. When the law is being broken, you get God's ordained authorities involved to help you. If your physical well-being (or that of your children) is in danger, we encourage you to appeal to your church leadership for protection, counsel, and help and go to the local authorities if necessary (Rom. 13:1). God has placed authorities in our lives for our protection—if necessary, please place yourself under their authority and seek their help.

One man repented, and one didn't. Their reaction wasn't Abigail's responsibility. Her responsibility was to be the woman that God wanted her to be in both those men's lives. That's to be our focus as well—to be women who place our ultimate trust in God and live as He calls us to in our current circumstances. When we do, God can use us to impact not only the Nabals in our life but also the world.

Dive Deeper into God's Word
Read Philippians 4:2–9.

Who was having conflict in this passage?

_____

_____

This passage may be very familiar to you. Does knowing that Paul wrote it to people in a difficult relational conflict change your perspective on it? How?

_____

_____

_____

Under each command from our passage, write one way you can do it this week.

Rejoice in the Lord always.

_____

Let your reasonableness be known to everyone.

_____

Do not be anxious about anything.

_____

Let your requests be made known to God by prayer and supplication with thanksgiving.

_____

Think about true, honorable, just, pure, lovely, commendable, excellent, and praiseworthy things.

_____

Practice what you have learned, received, heard, and seen.

_____

Day 5: TAKE IT HOME. MAKE IT PERSONAL.

Read Matthew 5:44–45.

Can you think of a time when you felt like praying for God's judgment on wicked people? How can you pray for those people today in a way that is glorifying to God?

_____

_____

_____

Knowing that Jesus gives us an eternal "happily-ever-after" is helpful when we endure suffering, but it can be hard to remember in the midst of hardship. What are some practical ways you can live out this truth as you go about your daily activities?

_____

_____

_____

_____

_____

Write down what God has taught you through this week's study, including any actions He wants you to take or insights He wants you to apply to your life.

_____

_____

_____

_____

Dive Deeper into God's Word
Read Philippians 4:2–13.

Our Philippians passage deals with the way that we think in suffering and conflict. Read the statements below, and let the Holy Spirit search your heart. Circle yes or no according to what He reveals.

Yes / No   I usually choose to rejoice in difficult circumstances.

Yes / No   I give my anxiety about my circumstances to God.

Yes / No   I often ask God to intervene in my circumstances.

Yes / No   When I pray about my situation, I tend to give thanks.

Yes / No   I often experience an unexplainable sense of God's peace and presence.

Yes / No   My thoughts focus on the Truth of God's Word, not my circumstances.

Yes / No   I trust that God will provide for my needs, and I'm content.

Yes / No   I usually choose obedience, even when I'm feeling discouraged.

Thinking rightly can be difficult when things are tough. For the statements next to which you circled "No," why do you think that's the case? Are there any questions (or even strong emotions) that you're wrestling with?

_____

_____

_____

Now, like our passage instructs, take those thoughts, emotions, and questions to the Lord. Give thanks that He offers you peace and His presence. Be honest about your failure to obey His Word and the reasons it's hard for you. Ask Him to help you focus on His Truth and be obedient, even when your circumstances are difficult. He is faithful to do it!

Jesus, I ask that all those who do not know You as their Savior would be brought to repentance, no matter what it takes. Help me to have an eternal perspective on both my circumstances and the current events of the world. Help me to live for Your glory as I wait for You to bring a truly happy ending to my story.

HELP ME TO have an eternal PERSPECTIVE on both my CIRCUMSTANCES and the current EVENTS OF THE world

Spend time meditating on and memorizing the following verse this week:

BELOVED, DO NOT BE SURPRISED AT THE FIERY TRIAL WHEN IT COMES UPON YOU TO TEST YOU, AS THOUGH SOMETHING STRANGE WERE HAPPENING TO YOU. BUT REJOICE INSOFAR AS YOU SHARE CHRIST'S SUFFERINGS, THAT YOU MAY ALSO REJOICE AND BE GLAD

When HIS GLORY is Revealed

1 PETER 4:12–13

Week 6

Introduction

As we have looked at Abigail's story in detail over the last few weeks, perhaps you've found yourself resonating with her. Can you identify any of the characters in her story in your own life? Which one are you? Has your perspective of that person or situation changed as you see them through this passage of Scripture?

Jesus Is the Better David

During our study of Abigail's life, we've focused in on David, who was, in many ways, Israel's greatest king. God promised David that an heir, an even greater king, would sit on his throne forever (2 Sam. 7:12–16). And who was that heir? Our Lord Jesus! Check out how He showed Himself to be greater than Israel's best earthly king.

Jesus . . .

- Is both the root and descendant of David (Rev. 22:16).
- Fulfilled prophecy and the promises to David (John 7:42).
- Is David's Lord (Acts 2:25–28).
- Is God's Son and David's heir (Rom. 1:3).
- Is the Christ (Acts 2:36; John 7:42).
- Is the Savior (Luke 2:11).
- Brings forgiveness of sins and freedom (Acts 13:38–39).
- Had mercy on the suffering and worked miracles (Luke 18:35–43; Matt. 15:21–28).
- Is Lord of the Sabbath (Luke 6:1–5).
- Was raised from the dead and did not see corruption (Acts 13:36–37; 2 Tim. 2:8).
- Sits on David's throne (Luke 1:32).
- Is exalted at the right hand of God (Acts 2:33).
- Has the key of the kingdom (Rev. 3:7).
- Has conquered (Rev. 5:5)!

While we have learned practical ways of dealing with difficult people and circumstances with grace and wisdom, the story of Abigail also points to the bigger picture of glorifying God through and despite tough situations. It challenges us to examine our hearts in light of the hardships we currently face and to place our hope in the eternal life that is coming. Because of this promise and through the power of the Holy Spirit, we can respond well to those people who make life complicated.

Day 1: PUTTING IT ALL TOGETHER

Do a quick skim to review 1 Samuel 25.

The small peek we got into the life of Abigail is a powerful and challenging one. This woman lived in an extremely difficult situation, married to a man whose name literally meant "fool" and who personified that meaning. But throughout 1 Samuel 25, Abigail remained calm, responded to foolishness with wisdom, and trusted in the Lord to take care of her.

We will all encounter our own foolish and difficult people to deal with at some point. Although Abigail's example doesn't give us all the answers we need, it does provide practical insight about how to deal with others.

As we wrap up, let's go back and answer the questions raised at the beginning of our study, as well as review what we've learned over the last six weeks.

As we look at Nabal, Abigail, and David, what examples do you find to either be followed or avoided?

_____

_____

_____

_____

What do 1 Samuel 25 and Nabal, Abigail, and David teach you about the heart, the ways, and the character of God?

_____

_____

_____

How do 1 Samuel 25 and Nabal, Abigail, and David point you to Jesus and the gospel?

_____

_____

_____

How would you summarize what the story of Abigail teaches you about dealing with the fools in your life?

_____

_____

_____

What is one thing God has shown you about your own responses as a result of this study?

_____

_____

_____

_____

_____

Read or listen to 1 Peter.

We looked at 1 Peter 2 and 3 during week one of our study. In this last week, we'll be looking at chapter 4. Today, read (or listen to) the entire book of 1 Peter, and write down the following:

What is one thing I learn about Jesus from this book?

_____

What is one command the Lord is calling me to obey from this book?

_____

What is one promise from this book I can hold onto?

_____

List any other thoughts you have about this book and how its truth speaks into your circumstances.

_____

_____

_____

Day 2: AN EXTREME SITUATION

Read Philippians 1:9–10.

Throughout 1 Samuel 25, we've seen some examples of extreme reactions. Nabal's insulting response to David's reasonable request was offensive and disparaging. David's response to strap on his sword and prepare to retaliate was over the top.

When treated badly, we often go to extremes as well. Sometimes we lash out in anger, which can have disastrous results. Or instead of dealing openly with the issues, we remain silent and allow bitterness to develop in our hearts. How do you usually respond when someone hurts you? Place an "x" to show where you normally fall on this continuum.

LASH OUT IN ANGER   DISCUSS HONESTLY   IGNORE THE PROBLEM

REFUSE TO FORGIVE   OFFER FORGIVENESS   HARBOR BITTERNESS

Abigail didn't go to an extreme. What do you admire most about the ways Abigail responded?

_____

_____

If we want that same kind of wisdom in our interactions and relationships with others, it's necessary to continually cry out to the Lord to direct our life. We can't rely on our own understanding or act based on our emotions. Instead, we can act on the Truth of God's Word and follow the direction of the Holy Spirit in knowing what to do and how and when to do it. Not only will following this pattern protect us from saying all kinds of things we'll regret later, it can also help to defuse the situation and safeguard relationships.

How has listening to the direction of the Holy Spirit protected you from reacting unwisely when people have treated you badly?

_____

_____

What can you do today to help you better listen to the prompting of the Holy Spirit in future situations?

_____

_____

_____

Read 1 Peter 4.

Does this passage add anything new to what you have studied and learned through this study? About Jesus or about how to handle relationships and suffering?

_____

_____

_____

_____

Paul gives a list of behaviors that "the Gentiles" (unbelievers) do in verse 3. Do you tend to do any of these things to help deal with your circumstances?

_____

_____

In contrast, verse 1 encourages us to think like Jesus. Based on what you've learned throughout this study, what would it look like to have the mind of Christ as you deal with difficult people? How can you turn from your passions to instead embrace Christ's thinking?

_____

_____

Day 3: A PROPER RESPONSE

Read Colossians 3:12–14.

Part of the reason that Abigail's story is so beneficial is that it's not unrealistic. We don't walk away with the expectation that if we're a godly woman like Abigail, then all the foolish people in our lives will immediately turn and repent. Nabal never repented. He refused the grace and the mercy of God that were available to him.

Even in the midst of her sorrow over her husband's rebellion against the Lord and ultimate death, Abigail could sleep at night knowing that she wasn't the one who provoked him. Nabal made his own choices, and God dealt with him.

So many relationships get into trouble when we respond like Nabal to Nabals. When somebody acts like a fool, we often think, *Two can play this game*, and then end up doing and saying things we regret.

Turmoil is the end result of these actions rather than peace. Plus, that moment where God could use us in turning that person's heart is gone. Abigail was instrumental in changing David's actions. In that case, because he had a heart for God, her wisdom and approach were effective. But if you take up your sword to retaliate, you're missing an opportunity God may have for you to be an instrument of repentance in someone else's life.

So often when we interact with difficult people, we feel as if we need to deal with the situation immediately. But another way to look at the situation is to take the long view—to realize that our life is bundled up in the Lord, and He is ultimately in control of the outcome.

When our emotions are involved, we feel violated and have this instinct to do whatever we have to do to make sure the other person sees that they're wrong. However, **we can win the battle but lose the war—and lose peace in our own soul in the process.** When we are in God's Word daily and allow the Holy Spirit to direct our words, we're letting God fulfill His purposes both in our life and the life of the other person.

Describe any unresolved issues between you and others. Are you harboring pain or unforgiveness because of their foolish choices?

_____

_____

_____

How does Colossians 3:12–14 relate to the situation you just described?

_____

_____

_____

What actions do you need to take in response to the situation? (Check all that apply.)

___ Get godly counsel from a pastor or elder at your church.

___ Discuss this area of hurt with the right person at the right time, in the right tone of voice.

___ Let the issue drop. Choose to let a minor offense go.

___ Choose to forgive and begin to heal from hurt and bitterness.

Dive Deeper into God's Word
Read 1 Peter 4:1–6.

How have you suffered because you chose to do good? How does verse 5 give you hope for that situation?

_____

_____

Ephesians 2:1 tells us that you were once dead. How was the gospel preached to you?

_____

_____

Of the difficult people in your life, who are "those who are dead" that need to hear the gospel? How can you live and speak the gospel into their lives?

_____

_____

_____

Day 4: THE WAY WE GROW

Read James 1:2–4.

Although none of us like it, growth usually requires some degree of pain. When we look back over the times we've grown spiritually the most, we can see that often those seasons were accompanied by problems and trials. God frequently uses suffering to teach us to become more like Him. In His sovereignty, God uses even the offenses and wrongs of others as part of the sanctification process in our own lives.

How has God used a painful time in your life to help you grow closer to Him?

_____

_____

_____

Remind yourself, what words were used to describe Nabal (1 Sam. 25:3)? What words were used to describe Abigail?

_____

_____

It seems amazing that Abigail survived years of marriage to this mean-spirited, ill-tempered man. But **what if she was beautiful and discerning not *in spite of* the harsh and ill-behaved man she had been married to *but because of* her relationship with him?** Was it her difficult circumstances that made her seek to know God and to become God's woman?

Because Scripture doesn't specifically tell us, we can't know for sure. However, one thing we do know—we cannot become like Christ apart from suffering. God perfected Christ through the things that He suffered (Heb. 2:10). **In our humanness, we want the glory and the end result of being like Christ without going through the process. But the process is the cross.** Your Nabal is your cross.

You can't become like Jesus without some type of suffering. There are no shortcuts to spiritual maturity. Growth often requires hurt and pain.

Read the following verses, and underline the phrases that refer to suffering.

> Although he [Jesus] was a son, he learned obedience through what he suffered. And being made perfect, he became the source of eternal salvation to all who obey him. (Heb. 5:8–9)

> If when you do good and suffer for it you endure, this is a gracious thing in the sight of God. For to this you have been called, because Christ also suffered for you, leaving you an example, so that you might follow in his steps. (1 Peter 2:20–21)

> Beloved, do not be surprised at the fiery trial when it comes upon you to test you, as though something strange were happening to you. But rejoice insofar as you share Christ's sufferings, that you may also rejoice and be glad when his glory is revealed. (1 Peter 4:12–13)

> We rejoice in our sufferings, knowing that suffering produces endurance, and endurance produces character, and character produces hope. (Rom. 5:3–4)

How does suffering give you the opportunity to be more like Jesus?

_____

_____

_____

Of all the four seasons, winter is generally the least favorite. Things are dark and cold. There's an absence of color, fewer signs of life. Everything seems dead.

But as the first signs of spring emerge, we rejoice. Trees bud and flowers bloom. Birds reappear, filling the air with their sweet songs. The death of winter has given way to new life!

Abigail went through a process of learning to live in a hard world and in a hard marriage. That is part of what made her the woman of God that we're talking about thousands of years later.

Whatever your circumstances, whether it's a person or a situation that's having a Nabal-like influence in your life, remember that God has a purpose in this. He wants to use it to make you into a woman who's wise and discerning. So let Him.

Don't run from the cross. Don't resist it. Don't resent it. Instead, embrace it. Because it's in the process of taking up that cross that God can shape you to be like Abigail—and ultimately, more like His Son.

Dive Deeper into God's Word
Read 1 Peter 4:7–11.

These verses give us another list of imperatives (commands). Fill in the chart below to help you apply them to your own situation.

OBEY BY...	TO WHOM...	BY DOING...
Responding with self-control		
Loving earnestly		
Showing hospitality		
Serving with my gifts		
Speaking truth		

According to verses 10 and 11, what does God give you to be able to obey these commands?

_____

_____

_____

What are the reasons given in this passage to do all of these things?

_____

_____

_____

Day 5: TAKE IT HOME. MAKE IT PERSONAL.

Read Revelation 21:1–6.

Are you currently going through a season of winter? What signs of new life (if any) are on the horizon? If not, ask God to help you endure until "spring comes."

_____

_____

_____

What are ways that you can embrace the cross in your current circumstances?

_____

_____

_____

_____

Write down what God has taught you through this week's study, including any actions He wants you to take or insights He wants you to apply to your life.

_____

_____

_____

Dive Deeper into God's Word
Read 1 Peter 4:12–19.

What have you found surprising about your current trials (v. 12)? Are there any practical ways you can turn that surprise into rejoicing (v. 13)? If you aren't able to think of any, write out a prayer and ask God to guide you in order to make rejoicing part of your everyday life.

_____

_____

_____

_____

_____

_____

_____

_____

_____

_____

_____

_____

_____

Consider: Have you ever suffered for wrongdoing? Did you feel shame? If you are suffering unjustly now (or have in the past) from a difficult person, does that bring you shame? God calls you not to be ashamed of your circumstances, but to glorify Him in them through trust and obedience. Journal any reflections about the role of shame in your suffering below. Then take it to the Lord in prayer.

_____

_____

_____

_____

_____

_____

Verse 19 reminds us that our Creator is faithful. In what ways has He shown that faithfulness to you through your circumstances and through this study? How can you entrust your soul to Him moving forward?

_____

_____

_____

_____

_____

_____

Thank You, Lord, for all that You've taught me through Abigail. Help me to take the lessons I've learned in the past six weeks and live them out as I deal with the difficult people in my life. Make me to be a wise and discerning woman who will draw others to You through my words and my example. Teach me to trust You throughout hard circumstances. May I learn to embrace the cross, as you shape me to be like Your Son, Jesus Christ.

THANK YOU, Lord, for all THAT YOU'VE taught me THROUGH Abigail

SMALL GROUP
DISCUSSION QUESTIONS

———

Week 1:

- Think of a time you let difficult people or circumstances be an excuse for your wrong behavior. How would remembering the character and promises of God have helped in the situation?
- While wealth and beauty are not intrinsically evil, what are some dangers of allowing them to hold a prominent place in your life?
- It's easy to read an account like this and think, *Don't be like Nabal; be like Abigail.* But we know Abigail isn't the true hero in this story—Jesus is. Where do you see Jesus in Abigail's words and actions? How does seeing God's grace at work in and through her give you hope for dealing with difficult people in your own life?

Week 2:

- What are some Nabal-like tendences you have, and what do they reveal about your heart?
- When convicted of sin, how can we know whether we're addressing the root problem or just dealing with surface issues? What does the Bible have to say regarding behavior modification versus a deep heart cleanse? (See Matthew 23:25–28; Luke 18:9–14; Matthew 15:1–20; John 15:4–5.)
- In this week's study, we saw multiple instances of rash, out-of-control behavior. What is a biblical way to handle a situation in which one or more people are acting irrationally? (Read Ephesians 4:31–32 if you need help.)
- Think of a time you put yourself in jeopardy by leaning on your own understanding. What were the consequences? How might they have been avoided? Do you have any ways of holding yourself accountable like the H.A.L.T. principle?
- What can you glean from Christ's example of dealing with difficult people? How did Jesus respond to injustice, anger, or betrayal?

SMALL GROUP DISCUSSION QUESTIONS

Week 3:

- What is your response to a crisis? Are you fearful? Passive? Quick-tempered? Discerning? How and why is Abigail's response one worth examining and emulating?
- Are wisdom and common sense the same thing? Why or why not?
- According to Scripture, how do you gain wisdom? (See James 1:5; Job 12:13, 28:28; Psalm 111:10; Proverbs 2:6–7.)
- How did you define submission? Do you see Abigail's actions as being submissive? Why or why not?
- How have you seen God at work in your own life—in your salvation story, through a blessing or miracle, or in the midst of a difficult situation?

Week 4:

- Why is it hard to wait on the Lord instead of taking matters into your own hands?
- You can't control others, but you can control yourself. Give an example of a time when using discretion and patience defused a volatile situation. How did you see God at work in both yourself and the other individual(s)?
- How do you live at peace with those who refuse to reconcile? What aspects of God's character bring you wisdom and comfort for handling challenging relationships?
- How does the example of Jesus, our Savior, influence the way you respond when treated unjustly? And how does it provide hope to your situation?

SMALL GROUP
DISCUSSION QUESTIONS

———

Week 5:

- Which of God's promises have given you assurance and helped you overcome temptation?
- What perspective does Scripture offer for when we're wrestling with doubts and questioning God's plans or timetable?
- What do you know to be true of God even when your prayers seemingly go unanswered?

Week 6:

- How do we know if we are keeping in step with the Spirit? What does Scripture teach about being filled with the Spirit? (See Romans 8:1–22; Galatians 5:16–26; Ephesians 5:1–21.)
- How can releasing your bitterness and extending forgiveness help to defuse a tense situation? Why is harboring bitterness detrimental not only to the offender but to the offended?
- How has God used suffering to transform you more into His likeness? Does knowing Christ also suffered bring you hope? Why or why not?
- What stood out to you the most about Abigail? David? Nabal? What have you learned or grown to love even more about God?

Notes

[1] Trent C. Butler, ed., *Holman Bible Dictionary* (Nashville: Holman Bible Publishers, 1991), 1227.

[2] "First Samuel," Insight for Living, accessed May 2, 2018, http://insight.org/resources/bible/the-historical-books/first-samuel.

[3] "Sheep-Shearing," StudyLight.org, *International Standard Bible Encyclopedia*. https://www.studylight.org/encyclopedias/isb/s/sheep-shearing.html, accessed May 2, 2018.

[4] "Sheep," StudyLight.org, The 1901 Jewish Encyclopedia, accessed May 2, 2018, https://www.studylight.org/encyclopedias/tje/s/sheep.html.

[5] Fred H. Wight, "Manners and Customs of Bible Lands," accessed May 2, 2018, http://www.baptistbiblebelievers.com/LinkClick. aspx?fileticket=lrVs01Bbg5k%3d&tabid=232&mid=762.

[6] Trent C. Butler, ed., *Holman Bible Dictionary* (Nashville: Holman Bible Publishers, 1991), 692.

[7] "Imprecatory Psalms," Bible Gateway, *Asbury Bible Commentary*, accessed May 2, 2018, https://www.biblegateway.com/resources/asbury-bible-commentary/Imprecatory-Psalms.

Reflections

Reflections

Reflections

Reflections

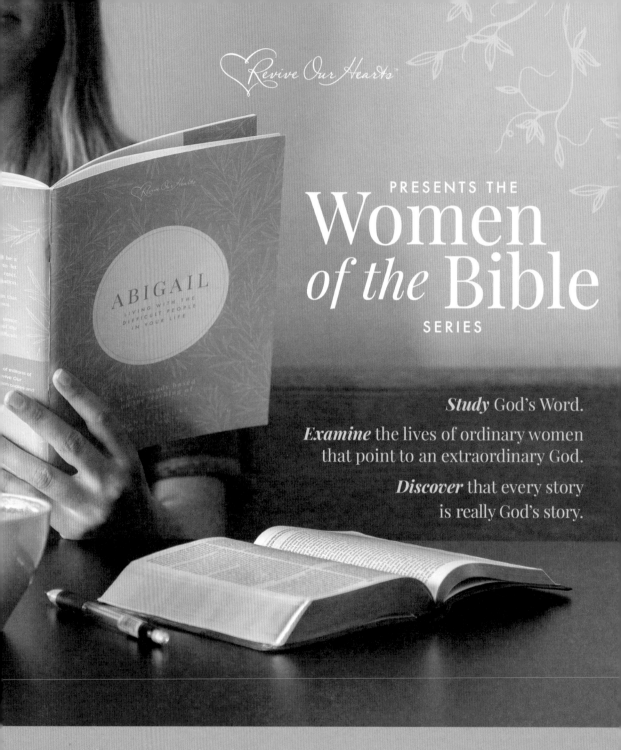

MORE FROM

Revive Our Hearts™

RADIO • EVENTS • BLOGS

LEADERS

REVIVE OUR HEARTS . COM